Dear Parents,

Welcome to the Scholastic Reader series. We have taken over 80 years of experience with teachers, parents, and children and put it into a program that is designe⌇⌇⌇⌇⌇ rests and skills.

Level 1—Short sentences ⌇ s kids can sound out using their p are important to remember.

Level 2—Longer sentences and stories with words kids need to know and new "big" words that they will want to know.

Level 3—From sentences to paragraphs to longer stories, these books have large "chunks" of texts and are made up of a rich vocabulary.

Level 4—First chapter books with more words and fewer pictures.

It is important that children learn to read well enough to succeed in school and beyond. Here are ideas for reading this book with your child:

- Look at the book together. Encourage your child to read the title and make a prediction about the story.
- Read the book together. Encourage your child to sound out words when appropriate. When your child struggles, you can help by providing the word.
- Encourage your child to retell the story. This is a great way to check for comprehension.
- Have your child take the fluency test on the last page to check progress.

Scholastic Readers are designed to support your child's efforts to learn how to read at every age and every stage. Enjoy helping your child learn to read and love to read.

—Francie Alexander
Chief Education Officer
Scholastic Education

For those I love most
(who can also make me the angriest!)
—CK

No part of this publication may be reproduced, or stored in a retrieval system, or transmitted in any form or by any means, electronic, mechanical, photocopying, recording, or otherwise, without written permission of the publisher. For information regarding permission, write to Scholastic Inc., Attention: Permissions Department, 557 Broadway, New York, NY 10012.

Text copyright © 2004 by Cecily Kaiser.
Illustrations copyright © 2004 by Cary Pillo.
Activities copyright © 2005 Scholastic Inc.
All rights reserved. Published by Scholastic Inc.
SCHOLASTIC, CARTWHEEL BOOKS, and associated logos
are trademarks and/or registered trademarks of Scholastic Inc.

Library of Congress Cataloging-in-Publication Data is available.

ISBN: 0-439-72998-X

20 19 18   40   10 11 12
Printed in the U.S.A. • This edition first printing, July 2005

IF YOU'RE ANGRY AND YOU KNOW IT!

by **Cecily Kaiser**

Illustrated by **Cary Pillo**

Scholastic Reader — Level 2

SCHOLASTIC INC.

New York Toronto London Auckland Sydney
Mexico City New Delhi Hong Kong Buenos Aires

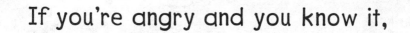

If you're angry and you know it,

STOMP YOUR FEET.

If you're angry and you know it,

STOMP YOUR FEET.

If you're angry and you know it,
and you really want to show it,
if you're angry and you know it,
STOMP YOUR FEET.

If you're angry and you know it,

BANG A DRUM.
If you're angry and you know it,
BANG A DRUM.

If you're angry and you know it,
and you really want to show it,
if you're angry and you know it,
BANG A DRUM.

If you're angry
and you know it,

WALK AWAY.

If you're angry and you know it,
WALK AWAY.

If you're angry and you know it,
and you really want to show it,
if you're angry and you know it,
WALK AWAY.

If you're angry and you know it,

TAKE DEEP BREATHS.

If you're angry and you know it,

TAKE DEEP BREATHS.

If you're angry and you know it,
and you really want to show it,
if you're angry and you know it,
TAKE DEEP BREATHS.

If you're angry and you know it,

TELL A FRIEND.

If you're angry and you know it,
TELL A FRIEND.

If you're angry and you know it,
and you really want to show it,
if you're angry and you know it,
TELL A FRIEND.

Then...
You're happy and you know it,
once again!

Then you're happy and you know it,
once again!

Then you're happy and you know it,

you're not angry and you show it,

Then you're happy and you know it,
once again!

Dear Parents and Teachers,

Anger is a normal and inevitable human emotion. Yet not one of us was born knowing how and when to express *our* aggressive feelings in a socially acceptable and emotionally productive way. So, it is our responsibility, as educators and role models, to help our children learn the best way to handle all their feelings.

The primary message of this book is: When you're angry, it's good to know it. At first, children may show their anger physically, by stomping their feet or banging a drum, as long as no one gets hurt. But it is even better for them to learn to "walk away" (leave the scene), or "take deep breaths" (do whatever it is that helps them to calm down). And perhaps the most productive way of handling anger is to share their feelings with a friend or grown-up whom they trust. Strong feelings can be communicated in many ways, such as through shared pretend play, through drawing, or through telling a story to an empathetic listener.

Anger is as natural as joy, excitement, or any other emotion. However, the way in which anger is addressed can be either detrimental or productive for a child's social development. Children who learn to identify and cope with their strong feelings are most likely to go on to lead healthier, more joyful lives, and contribute to a more peaceful world.

Adele M. Brodkin, Ph.D.
Senior Child Development Consultant to Scholastic Inc.